JOYFUL MYSTERIES
A Rosary Guide for Children

Gianna Martin

copyright © 2019 Gianna Martin

For Gus, Louise, Tommy, and Bug

HOW TO USE THIS BOOK:

"LET THE LITTLE CHILDREN COME TO ME, AND DO NOT HINDER THEM, FOR THE KINGDOM OF GOD BELONGS TO SUCH AS THESE" MARK 10:14.

Children often surprise us with their spiritual depth. The goal of this book is to bring that depth to the Rosary, even before our tots are able to recite the prayers with us. This book is best read with an adult's guidance to encourage familial participation and reflection. There are even discussion questions for before and after prayer, designed to address the four elements of prayer (adoration, confession, thanksgiving, and petitions) and reflect contemplative scriptural reading. With your help, prayer will come alive for your children and plant the seeds of faith, hope, and love. God bless, and have fun!

QUESTIONS TO ASK BEFORE READING:

What do you know about God?

What are you thankful for today?

What are you sorry for today?

What do you want God to help you with today?

Who do you want to pray for today?

This is a Rosary.

We use a Rosary to help us pray.

Praying a Rosary helps us focus on the stories of Jesus' life.

We wonder how Mary felt and acted in these stories.

We count the beads of the Rosary
to keep track of our prayers.

1 2 3 4 5 6 7 8 9 10

The Rosary begins with the Sign of the Cross and the Apostle's Creed.

This reminds us of what we believe in.

The Apostles' Creed can teach us a lot about our faith!

The adults praying with you can answer any questions you have.

Next we pray an Our Father, three Hail Marys, and a Glory Be prayer.
We ask God to help us have:

Faith   Hope   Charity

Now, we are ready to think about the stories of Jesus' life!

THE FIRST JOYFUL MYSTERY: THE ANNUNCIATION

God sent the angel Gabriel to ask Mary to be Jesus' mother. She said yes! Mary, help me to always say yes to whatever God wants me to do.

THE SECOND JOYFUL MYSTERY: THE VISITATION

Mary travelled to her cousin Elizabeth. When Elizabeth saw Mary, her own baby named John leapt with joy in her womb. Both Elizabeth and John were excited to meet Jesus. Mary, help me to share God with my neighbors.

● ● ● ● ● ● ● ● ● ● ●

THE THIRD JOYFUL MYSTERY: THE NATIVITY

Mary gave birth to Jesus in a manger. Mary, Joseph, angels, shepherds and kings sang praises to Jesus that night because they loved him so much. Mary, help me to love Jesus more!

THE FOURTH JOYFUL MYSTERY: THE PRESENTATION

One of God's laws was to bring any new babies to the Temple in Jerusalem. Mary and Joseph took Jesus to the Temple to offer Him to God. There, they met a holy man named Simeon that blessed Jesus and said He would be the savior of the world! Mary, help us to follow God's law.

THE FIFTH JOYFUL MYSTERY: THE FINDING AT THE TEMPLE

When Jesus was twelve, Mary and Joseph didn't know where Jesus was. After looking for three days, they found Jesus in the Temple, teaching the leaders there. Mary and Joseph were very glad to find Jesus again. Mary, help me to never be separated from Jesus!

The Rosary ends with a Hail Holy Queen prayer and a St. Michael prayer.

We ask for God to forgive us, guide us, and protect us with the help of Mary and St. Michael the Archangel.

I love praying the Rosary with you. I can't wait to do it again!

Until next time, remember:
God loves you very much!

QUESTIONS TO ASK AFTER READING:

Who is your favorite person in the stories? What do you like about them?

What do you think was the happiest part of the book?

What part do you want to know more about?

What questions do you have about prayer? About the Rosary? About God?

Made in United States
North Haven, CT
27 April 2023

35936314R00015